TECHNOLOGY

YOU CAN TASTE

JESSIE ALKIRE

Consulting Editor, Diane Craig, MA/Reading Specialist

Super Sandcastle

An Imprint of Abdo Publishing
abdobooks.com

ABDOBOOKS.COM

Published by Abdo Publishing, a division of ABDO, PO Box 398166, Minneapolis, Minnesota 55439. Copyright © 2019 by Abdo Consulting Group, Inc. International copyrights reserved in all countries. No part of this book may be reproduced in any form without written permission from the publisher. Super SandCastle™ is a trademark and logo of Abdo Publishing.

Printed in the United States of America, North Mankato, Minnesota
102018
012019

THIS BOOK CONTAINS RECYCLED MATERIALS

Design: Emily O'Malley, Mighty Media, Inc.
Production: Mighty Media, Inc.
Editor: Liz Salzmann
Cover Photographs: Mighty Media, Inc.; Shutterstock
Interior Photographs: iStockphoto; Library of Congress; Mighty Media, Inc.; Shutterstock

The following manufacturers/names appearing in this book are trademarks: Bates National Rule™, Betty Crocker™, Essential Everyday®, Haribo® Starmix™, Life Savers®, Makey Makey®, PAM®, Pillsbury Creamy Supreme®, Pringles®, Reynolds®, Sharpie®

Library of Congress Control Number: 2018948861

Publisher's Cataloging-in-Publication Data
Names: Alkire, Jessie, author.
Title: Technology you can taste / by Jessie Alkire.
Description: Minneapolis, Minnesota : Abdo Publishing, 2019 | Series: Super simple science you can snack on
Identifiers: ISBN 9781532117275 (lib. bdg.) | ISBN 9781532170133 (ebook)
Subjects: LCSH: Technology--Juvenile literature. | Cooking--Juvenile literature. | Science--Experiments--Juvenile literature. | Gastronomy--Juvenile literature.
Classification: DDC 641.0--dc23

Super SandCastle™ books are created by a team of professional educators, reading specialists, and content developers around five essential components—phonemic awareness, phonics, vocabulary, text comprehension, and fluency—to assist young readers as they develop reading skills and strategies and increase their general knowledge. All books are written, reviewed, and leveled for guided reading and early reading intervention programs for use in shared, guided, and independent reading and writing activities to support a balanced approach to literacy instruction.

TO ADULT HELPERS

The projects in this book are fun and simple. There are just a few things to remember to keep kids safe. Some projects require the use of sharp or hot objects. Also, kids may be using messy ingredients. Make sure they protect their clothes and work surfaces. Review the projects before starting, and be ready to assist when necessary.

KEY SYMBOLS

Watch for these warning symbols in this book. Here is what they mean.

HOT!
You will be working with something hot. Get help!

SHARP!
You will be working with something sharp. Get help!

CONTENTS

WHAT IS TECHNOLOGY?

The word *technology* has many different meanings. One meaning is "the use of science to invent useful things or to solve problems." These inventions and **solutions** are also often called technologies.

Many early technologies were invented during the **Industrial Revolution**. This was a time of great progress in the 1700s and 1800s. Large factories were built to make **textiles**, metals, and more.

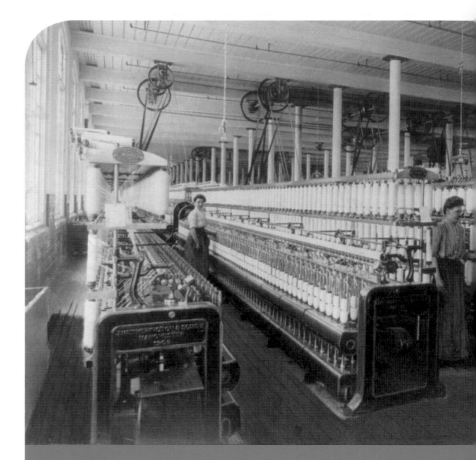

BY THE 1900S, IMPROVED SPINNING AND WEAVING TECHNOLOGIES HAD LED TO LARGE TEXTILE FACTORIES.

IN THE 1800S, STEAM-POWERED TRAINS CARRIED GOODS AND PEOPLE ALL OVER EUROPE AND THE UNITED STATES.

One important technology at this time was the steam engine. Steam technologies were first used in the late 1600s and early 1700s.

In 1765, James Watt improved on the steam engine. Steam engines were later used to power factories, trains, boats, and more.

TECHNOLOGY TODAY

Today's technologies include computers, smartphones, and other electronics. These devices help people and businesses succeed. They can also provide entertainment!

SELF-DRIVING CARS

Many companies are working to create self-driving cars. These cars can operate without human drivers. Many people think these cars could be safer than those driven by humans.

WAYMO SELF-DRIVING CARS ARE MADE BY TECHNOLOGY COMPANY GOOGLE.

SOLAR ROOFS

Companies like Tesla and Dow are creating roofs made of tiny **solar panels**. These roofs look just like normal roofs. But they use the sun's energy to power homes and businesses!

ROBOTS

Scientists have been building robots since the early 1900s. But robot technology has advanced quickly in the past few years. Sophia is a humanlike robot. It was built by the company Hanson Robotics in 2015. Sophia can walk, talk, recognize people, and more.

SOPHIA THE ROBOT

TECHNOLOGY SNACKS

You can learn a lot about technology by making the fun snacks in this book!

GET READY

* Ask an adult for **permission** to use kitchen tools and ingredients.

* Read the snack's list of tools and ingredients. Make sure you have everything you need.

* Does a snack require ingredients you don't like? Get creative! Find other ingredients you enjoy instead.

SNACK CLEAN & SAFE

* Clean your work surface before you start.

* Wash your hands before you work with food.

* Keep your work area tidy. This makes it easier to find what you need.

* Ask an adult for help when handling sharp or hot objects.

CLEANING UP

* Don't waste unused ingredients! Store leftover ingredients to use later.

* Clean your work surface. Wash any dishes or tools you used.

* Wash your hands before you eat your snack!

INGREDIENTS & TOOLS

INGREDIENTS

CHOCOLATE FROSTING

CRISPY RICE CEREAL

FOOD COLORING

GRAHAM CRACKERS

GUMMY CANDIES

LIFE SAVERS HARD CANDIES

MARSHMALLOWS

MINI MARSHMALLOWS

MUFFIN MIX

NON-STICK COOKING SPRAY

ORANGES

PRE-COOKED HOT DOGS

SMALL PRETZEL STICKS

TWIZZLERS PULL 'N' PEEL CANDY

VANILLA FROSTING

HERE ARE SOME OF THE INGREDIENTS AND TOOLS YOU WILL NEED TO MAKE THE SNACKS IN THIS BOOK.

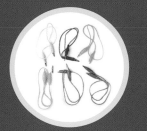

ALLIGATOR CABLES

BAKING PAN

COTTON SWABS

CRAFT KNIFE

CUTTING BOARD

5MM LEDS

FOIL MUFFIN CUPS

MAKEY MAKEY CLASSIC KIT

MICROWAVE-SAFE BOWL

PLASTIC WRAP

PLASTIC ZIPPER BAGS

PRINGLES CAN

SPATULA

WOODEN SKEWERS

ZINC NAILS

TOOLS

CANDY CIRCUIT

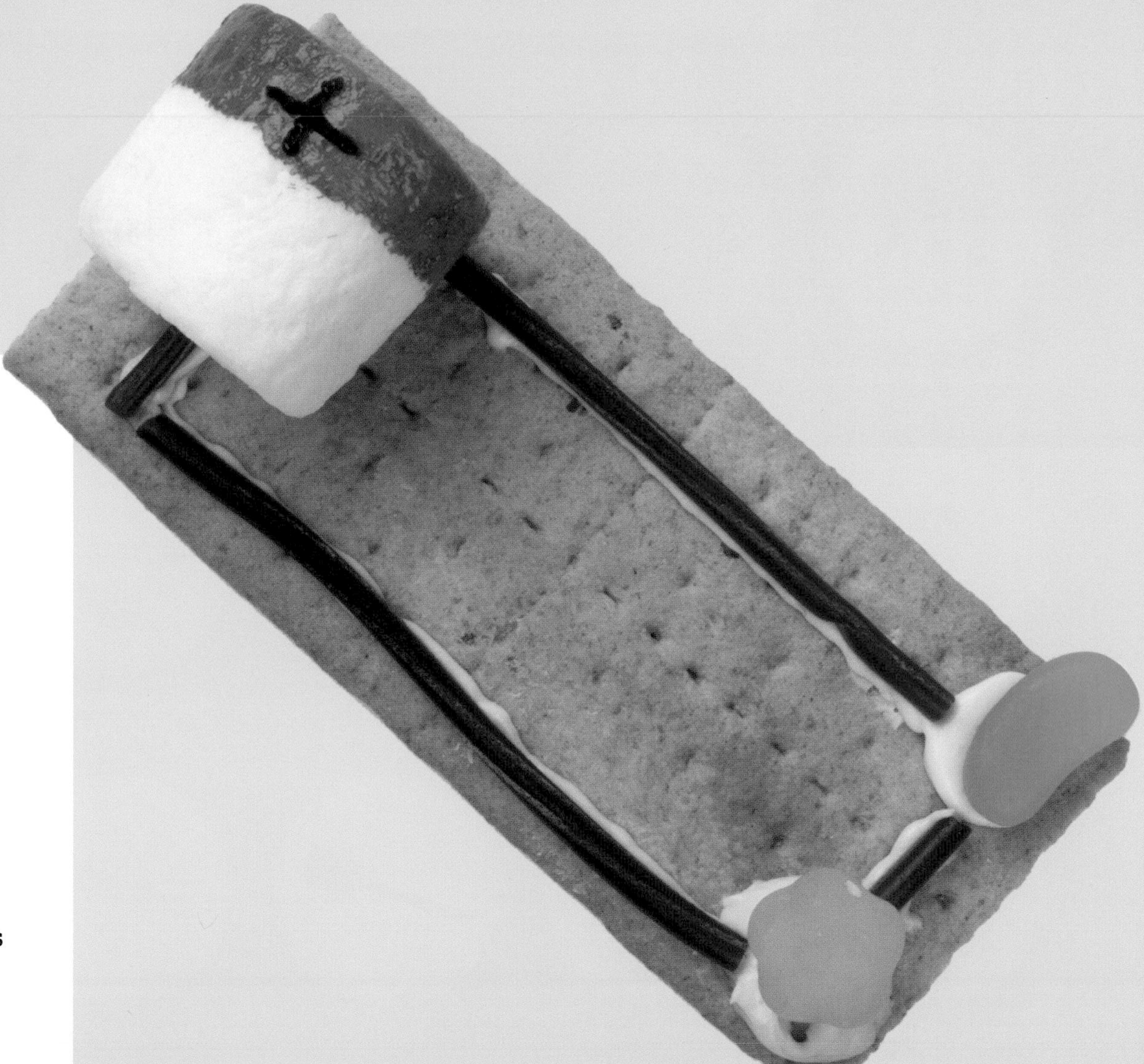

INGREDIENTS

- large marshmallow
- food coloring
- chocolate & vanilla frosting
- small pretzel sticks
- gummy candies
- graham cracker
- Twizzlers Pull 'n' Peel candy

TOOLS

- cotton swab
- 2 plastic zipper bags
- scissors
- ruler
- plate

A circuit is a closed path of electricity. It is the basis of every electric device. You can make your own model of a circuit with candy and graham crackers!

1. Dip the cotton swab into food coloring. Use the swab to color one end of the marshmallow.

2. Put a spoonful of chocolate frosting in a plastic bag. Seal the bag. Cut one corner of the bag to make a small hole.

3. Gently **squeeze** the bag until frosting comes out of the hole. Use it to draw a plus sign on the colored section of the marshmallow. The marshmallow is the **battery**.

4. Break off two ½-inch pieces of pretzel stick. Push one end of each pretzel piece into the bottom of a gummy candy. This is an **LED**.

5. Place a graham cracker on a plate. The graham cracker is the circuit board.

6. Repeat step 2 to make a bag of vanilla frosting.

Continued on the next page.

13

8

9

11

7. Put a large dot of frosting near one end of the graham cracker. Press the marshmallow onto the frosting.

8. Put a small dot of frosting near a corner of the cracker opposite the marshmallow. Press a gummy candy into the frosting. This is the circuit board switch.

9. Put another small dot of frosting next to the circuit board switch. Press the **LED** into the frosting so it is standing on the pretzel pieces.

10. Draw a line of vanilla frosting from the white end of the **battery** to the LED.

11. Draw a line of frosting between the LED and the switch. Draw a line from the switch to the dyed end of the battery.

12. Pull a rope of candy off a Twizzler. Cut the candy rope into lengths that fit on top of the frosting lines. Press the candy onto the lines. The Twizzlers rope is the wire.

13. Your circuit model is complete. If it were a real circuit, you could flip the switch to connect the circuit and light up the LED.

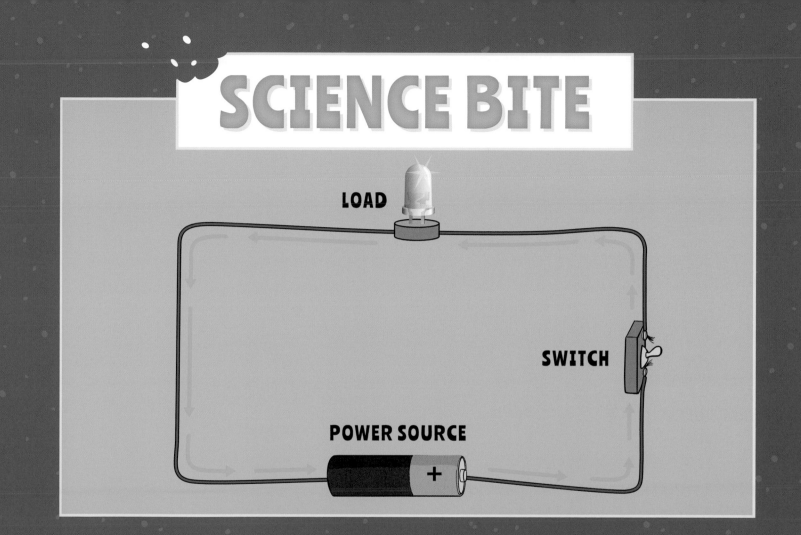

LOAD

SWITCH

POWER SOURCE

A CIRCUIT IS A CLOSED PATH THAT ELECTRICITY CAN TRAVEL THROUGH. A CIRCUIT USUALLY INCLUDES A POWER SOURCE, A SWITCH, AND A LOAD, SUCH AS A LIGHT BULB. THESE PARTS ARE CONNECTED BY WIRES.

WHEN THE SWITCH IS OFF, THE CIRCUIT IS BROKEN AND ELECTRICITY CAN'T REACH THE LOAD. TURNING ON THE SWITCH COMPLETES THE CIRCUIT. THIS ALLOWS THE ELECTRICITY TO REACH THE LOAD.

CITRUS BATTERY ⊘

INGREDIENTS
- 2 oranges

TOOLS
- sharp knife
- cutting board
- pennies
- zinc nails
- dish soap
- ruler
- 5 alligator cables
- 5 mm LED

Inside a **battery** are two metals surrounded by acid. You can use oranges, pennies, and nails to make an **edible** battery!

1. Have an adult help you cut the oranges in half. Wash the pennies and nails with soap and water.

2. Stick a penny halfway into the cut side of each orange half.

3. Stick a **zinc** nail into the cut side of each orange half. The nail and penny in each orange half should be about 1 inch (2.5 cm) apart.

4. Place the orange halves in a row.

5. Clip one end of an alligator cable to the nail in the first orange. The clip should connect to the nail where the nail meets the fruit.

Continued on the next page.

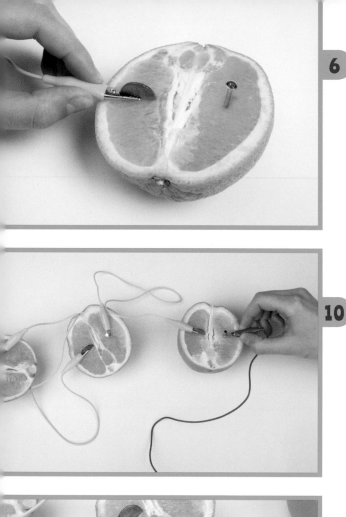

6. Clip the other end of the alligator cable to the penny in the next orange. The clip should connect to the penny where the penny meets the fruit.

7. Use another alligator cable to connect the nail in the second orange to the penny in the third.

8. Use the third alligator cable to connect the nail in the third orange to the penny in the fourth.

9. Clip one end of the fourth alligator cable to the penny in the first orange.

10. Clip one end of the fifth alligator cable to the nail in the fourth orange.

11. Clip the unconnected end of the fourth alligator cable to one of the **LED** wires. Clip the unconnected end of the fifth alligator cable to the other LED wire.

12. Watch what happens! The LED should light up. If it doesn't, make sure the alligator cables are all connected properly. You can also try switching which LED wires the alligator cables are clipped to.

SCIENCE BITE

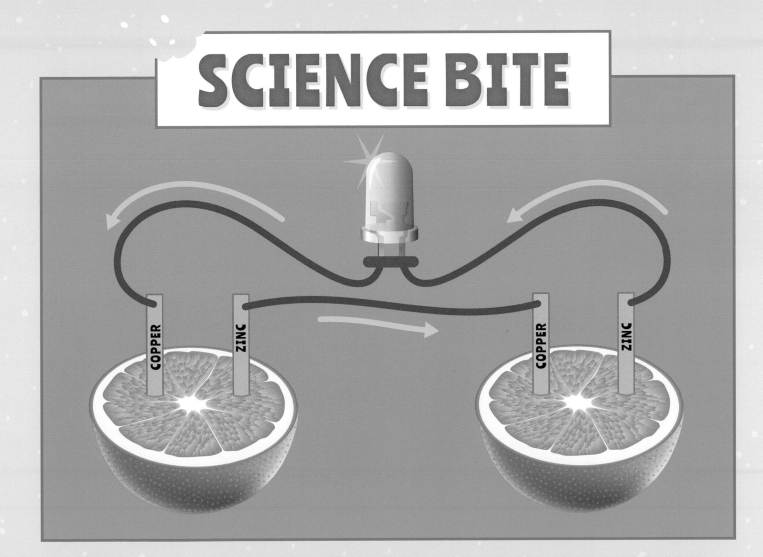

COPPER ZINC COPPER ZINC

THE ORANGE BATTERY USES TWO METALS. THE PENNIES ARE COPPER. THE NAILS ARE ZINC. THERE IS ACID IN THE FRUIT. THE ACID CREATES AN ELECTRIC CURRENT BETWEEN THE ZINC AND THE COPPER. WHEN THE ALLIGATOR CABLES ARE CONNECTED TO THE LED, THE CIRCUIT IS COMPLETE AND THE CURRENT MOVES THROUGH THE WIRES TO THE LED. THE LED LIGHTS UP!

MAGNIFICENT MUFFIN DRUM SET

INGREDIENTS

- muffin mix and ingredients

TOOLS

- bowl
- spoon
- muffin pan or foil muffin cups
- oven mitts
- Makey Makey Classic kit (includes USB cable, board, and alligator cables)
- dish soap
- paper towels
- computer

Makey Makey is an invention kit that lets everyday objects interact with computers. Try using Makey Makey to turn yummy muffins into a drum set!

1. Have an adult help you bake the muffins according to the instructions on the package.

2. Let the muffins cool completely.

3. Remove the muffins from the muffin pan or foil cups.

4. **Plug** the small end of the **USB** cable into the back of the Makey Makey board.

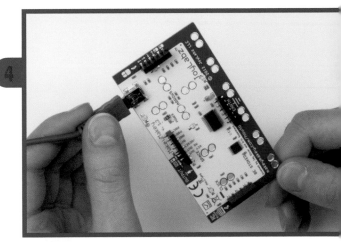

5. Plug the other end of the USB cable into the USB port on your computer. Close any pop-up windows that open.

6. Wash the ends of the alligator cables with soap and water. Dry them thoroughly.

Continued on the next page.

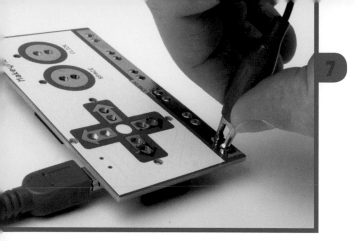

7

8

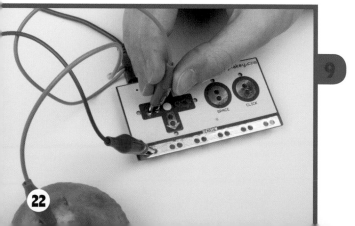

9

7. Clip one end of an alligator cable to the Earth bar on the Makey Makey board. Don't clip the other end to anything.

8. Stick one end of a second alligator cable into a muffin.

9. Connect the other end of the second alligator cable to the left arrow key on the Makey Makey board.

10. Stick one end of a third alligator cable into another muffin.

11. Connect the other end of the third alligator cable to the space bar key on the Makey Makey board.

12. Go to https://makeymakey.com/bongos/ on your computer.

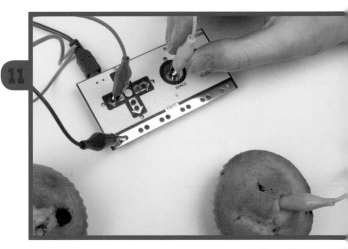

13. Hold the free end of the alligator cable that is connected to the Earth bar. With your other hand, lightly tap the sides of the muffins to play your muffin drum set!

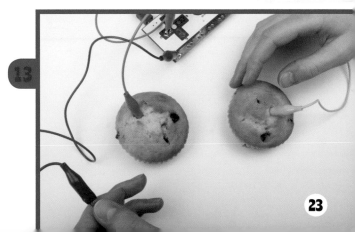

RICE KRISPY CAR ⊙

INGREDIENTS

- non-stick cooking spray
- 1 10-oz. bag mini marshmallows
- 4 tablespoons butter
- 6 cups crispy rice cereal
- small pretzel sticks
- Life Savers hard candies
- mini M&M's
- frosting
- Twizzlers Pull 'n' Peel candy

TOOLS

- large microwave-safe bowl
- spatula
- oven mitts
- 9 × 13 baking pan
- dinner knife
- ruler
- scissors

The automobile was one of the most important technological advancements in history. And new improvements are made every year. Try building a car with cereal and marshmallows.

1. Spray the bowl and spatula with non-stick cooking spray. Put the marshmallows and butter in the bowl.

2. Heat the bowl in the microwave for 30 seconds. Stir. Repeat until the marshmallow mixture is completely melted.

3. Gently stir the cereal into the marshmallow mixture.

4. Spray the baking pan with cooking spray.

5. Place the cereal mixture in the pan. Press the mixture into an even layer. Let it cool.

6. Cut out a cereal bar. It should be about 3 inches (8 cm) long and 2 inches (5 cm) wide. This is the body of the car.

Continued on the next page.

7

7. Place two pretzel sticks across the width of the car near each end. The pretzel sticks are the **axles**.

8. Turn the car over. Slide Life Saver candies onto the ends of each axle.

9. Cut out another cereal bar. Make it 2 inches (5 cm) wide and 1½ inches (4 cm) long. This is the cab of the car.

8

10. Set the cab on top of the body.

10

11. Press two mini M&M's onto the front of the car's body for **headlights**.

12. Spread some frosting onto the front of the car's cab.

13. Pull a candy rope off of a Twizzler. Cut three 1.5-inch (4 cm) pieces off the rope. Press the pieces onto the frosting so they cover the front of the cab. This is the car's **windshield**.

14. Set your car on a clean, flat, smooth surface. Push it forward and watch it move!

15. Cut additional marshmallow treat bars to make more cars. Try making the cars different shapes and sizes or using different snacks for some of the parts!

SOLAR HOT DOG COOKER ⊖

INGREDIENTS
- pre-cooked hot dogs

TOOLS
- Pringles can
- ruler
- marker
- craft knife
- hammer
- nail
- tape
- wooden skewer
- plastic wrap

Solar energy comes from the sun's heat. This can be used to heat buildings or even cook food. You can make a simple solar oven out of a Pringles can!

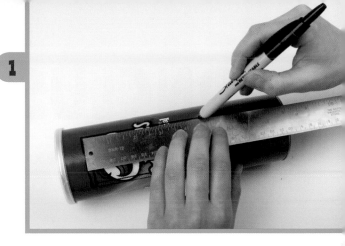

1. Draw a rectangle on the can. Make it 7 inches (18 cm) long and 2 inches (5 cm) wide.

2. Have an adult help you use a craft knife to cut out the rectangle. Have an adult help you use a hammer and nail to make a hole in the center of the can's lid and its bottom.

3. Set the can on its side with the opening facing up. Set the rectangle cutout so the can rests against it. Tape the rectangle in place.

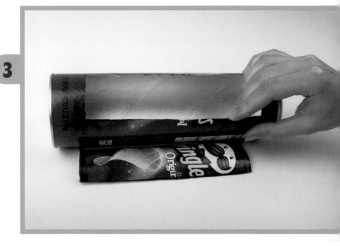

4. Push a clean skewer through the hot dog. Place the skewer in the can with the end sticking out of the hole in the bottom.

5. Place the lid on the can so the other end of the skewer sticks through the lid's hole.

6. Cover the opening in the can with plastic wrap. Tape the plastic wrap in place.

7. Place your solar oven outside in the sun for 1 to 2 hours. Then enjoy a warm hot dog for lunch!

CONCLUSION

Technology surrounds us every day. Scientists improve on old technologies to create new ones. Technology helps people and businesses succeed. It also provides entertainment!

MAKING SNACKS IS JUST ONE WAY TO LEARN ABOUT TECHNOLOGY. HOW WILL YOU CONTINUE YOUR TECHNOLOGY ADVENTURE?

QUIZ

1 WHEN DID THE INDUSTRIAL REVOLUTION OCCUR?

2 HANSON ROBOTICS' ROBOT IS NAMED SALLY. TRUE OR FALSE?

3 WHAT TRAVELS THROUGH A CIRCUIT?

LEARN MORE ABOUT IT!

YOU CAN FIND OUT MORE ABOUT TECHNOLOGY AT THE LIBRARY. OR YOU CAN ASK AN ADULT TO HELP YOU FIND INFORMATION ABOUT TECHNOLOGY ON THE INTERNET!

ANSWERS: 1. 1700S AND 1800S   2. FALSE   3. ELECTRICITY

GLOSSARY

axle – a bar that connects two wheels.

battery – a small container filled with chemicals that makes electrical power.

edible – safe to eat.

headlight – one of the two white lights on the front of a car, truck, or motorcycle.

Industrial Revolution – a period in England from about 1750 to 1850, when power-driven machinery started being used to make goods.

LED – a device that lights up when electricity passes through it.

load – something powered by an electrical circuit, such as a light or motor.

permission – when a person in charge says it's okay to do something.

plug – to stick the end of a cord into an outlet or other hole.

solar panel – a device that turns the sun's light into energy.

solution – an answer to, or a way to solve, a problem.

squeeze – to press the sides of something together.

textiles – woven or knit cloth.

USB – Universal Serial Bus. A system for connecting devices using a special kind of cord.

windshield – the window across the front of a car, truck, or motorcycle.

zinc – a bluish-white metallic element.